# The Gateway to Happi

# With Being Self-Aware

Mission Self-reset

7 Tips for a happy life

By Amouraj Kellett

I dedicate this book to

My children

Being a mother is the most difficult thing I have ever done in my life.

I have never professed that I am or have been the perfect mother

But I have always tried to be the best one I can be

I have tried to teach the right lessons and do the right thing

Even when I wasn't sure what the right thing was

I try to forgive myself over and over for doing things wrong

But most of all I have always loved you and always will.

See pictures on my website amouraj.co.uk

Website – Amouraj.co.uk

Facebook page – Mission Self-reset – unlock your potential

Other books by Amouraj Kellett

"A True Story of Love Loss and Survival (4 Sisters Battle Cancer)"

# CONTENT

# INTRODUCTION

1st January 2018.

It is a family tradition on the 1st January to have a brisk walk on the beach followed by fish and chips. This year was no exception. The sub-zero temperature coupled with a blustery gale made the fish and chips taste all the more delicious. The drive home consisted of various images of sleeping loved ones. Heads tilted back, heads slumped forward, mouth wide open, snoring baby grandson and my dog whiskey curled up warm under a blanket in the tailgate.

The blustery day was followed by an equally blustery evening. However, the open fire was burning bright and the atmosphere in our cottage was warm and cosy.

I was sitting comfortably on my bed, observing that the rain was not letting up at all, crashing against the bedroom window making such a racket, almost as if it was knocking to come in. Looking to the street light I quickly discovered that the sight of the rain was approaching cathartic. I began to reflect on the day and an exuberant Christmas with my family consisting of my husband, daughter 22, my son 25 and their partners along with my glorious gift of a grandson (two years old) and not forgetting as already mentioned, whiskey our loyal and loving pooch. We experienced our tummies filled to capacity with rich festive foods, toasting marshmallows on the open fire, having fun with Mason and his new friend "pop up pirate" (one of his Christmas toys). Christmas is such a time when as a family we are all in such high spirits.

I continued to sit snuggled on my bed, propped up by numerous pillows. I could now distinctly smell the oil burner, burning what was left of Christmas oil – the smell was Christmas pine trees, a perfectly serene atmosphere. Wow! A thought quickly infiltrated my mind. I was six years in remission from Breast Cancer, feeling dynamic and passionate about life, furthermore I had just secured a promotion at work which would commence on the 5$^{th}$ January. My career is in medical sales and as from the 5$^{th}$ would be a hospital specialist team leader in cardiovascular. It is the perfect profession for me in many ways and I am very passionate about it. The position requires a tremendous amount of self-discipline, motivation, commercial acumen and confidence but on the flip side I build close interesting relationships with cardiologists, manage my own time and most of all make a difference to the lives of patients. My background is in Psychology, obtaining a Psychology degree and being involved in various support groups, some of which I facilitated myself. In my spare time I write self-help books and a self-help blog (Amouraj.co.uk). I have penned a biography and recently started writing a passionate thriller novel. Should there possibly be any further spare time, a priority is to socialise with close friends (50 is the new 30), one of them my ever loving and fellow cancer surviving sister. Quality time with my family and generally embracing the diverse experiences of each day is a gift.

Do not get me wrong; I have my moments and my off days when to turn off my phone and hide away with mountains of chocolate would be the only solution to stop me being totally offensive to anyone who would dare to breath. You see we are all human!!

Believe me when I say, my life is a roller coaster ride; I am sure you feel the same otherwise you would not be reading this. I have periods of months at a time when all is going great, my spirits are high and then something kicks off and catches me off guard. I am forever fighting fires or placing all my ducks in a row and making sure they are happily waddling along. I have come to realise I want to *waddle in a line of ducks* with someone keeping me safe. Where do I apply?

Going back to my thoughts, sitting on the bed feeling content; this is such a contrast to eighteen months previous when I felt completely beaten down. At this time I had been four and half years pulling myself up from my treatment, experiencing and losing the battle to enjoy life. My guilt was enormous, guilt that I should be jumping with joy, shouting from the rooftops and dancing the jig. My two other sisters had lost their life to cancer and would swap with me any day of the week.

In a nutshell I was not embracing life, I was literally just getting through each day the best I could, literally dragging myself out of bed in the morning. After half an hour, my whole being was ready to get back in. It was a challenge to avoid any situation that would require energy. Family didn't really understand no matter how much I tried to enlighten them. My children were adults and brought their own problems and issues to the table, each problem draining me that much more. I didn't complain because I thought this is how it is –just get on with it. I had to put the little amount of energy I had into my job because that was what kept me going. My medication at the time brought with it many side effects (the side effects are mostly transient) one of which was bone pain, especially at night. I would be up and down all night trying to ignore it or taking painkillers hence the exhaustion. Unbeknown to me my Vitamin D levels were dangerously low, thankfully this was picked up. So, yes it was tough.

Knowing the two ends of the spectrum, I can sincerely declare, no matter how much people tell you, that you cannot get up one day deciding to be bright eyed and bushy tailed, no matter how much you crave it. You know how you want to feel but you just can't touch that feeling. It's like a bad itch that you cannot scratch. However it is possible to resume your zest for life; you just have to work for it.

My gruelling post cancer journey involved trial and error. A healthy attitude to my routine and restyling my thought patterns has brought me to a place of control, peace and being aware of my energy levels and feelings. These are not purely 'tips' for someone who is suffering post cancer fatigue; they are for you, you and you! My suggestions are for anyone who has missed the junction and is taking the unhappy road, the self-destructive lane or the path to despair.

Eighteen months ago when my physical and spiritual self were not in tune, I knew it was time to start living. In order for me to do this, I had to make some massive changes. Where would I start? Basically my objective was to restyle my approach to life. As I mentioned earlier, You can't just wake up one day and say "I am going to be my ideal self" Well, that's a lie, you can; however, to sustain your actions and feelings you need to break it down and look at what you want to work on and literally work on it.

I was on a busy work sales conference a couple of years ago. I cannot remember his name but the speaker was the guy who coached the successful cycling team to gold medals in the UK Olympics. One evening after the award ceremony and celebration dinner, it was a busy, noisy atmosphere. There were groups of colleagues scattered about perfecting their small talking skills. I was no exception, stood at the bar, having a conversation with the Olympic coach, probably boring him to death about how exhausted I was and could he give me any tips. He advised me – we can all be motivated to do things, we can be motivated to work towards our goals BUT it is commitment that will get you there and make you successful. Motivation can be short lived.

Initially I had to start with WHY? What had brought me to this point?

Still looking back to eighteen months ago, I remember one morning, sitting on the edge of my bed – my pooch was eyeballing me "Woof! Come on – I have dogs to sniff and balls to chase" - my husband had toddled off to work, totally oblivious to my emotional state of mind and my physical state of exhaustion. As far as he was concerned – I had my treatment and I was now fixed and ready to bounce my jolly self back to normality. If only it was that easy. The struggle I had with this was almost as bad as the treatment itself. My mind knew and remembered too well how I used to be, but my body would not comply at all. What was wrong with me?? I craved so much to jump out of bed and look forward to a fabulous day but my feet had other ideas. The side effects to my medication caused my feet to take longer to wake up than the rest of my body and I had to wait until *they* were ready to carry me. Consequently I was dangling them over the end of the bed. This was when I decided enough is enough – nothing was going to change unless I took control. I had accepted I was never going to be the person I was before but I sure as hell was not going down without a fight.

During my illness and treatment, my coping mechanism was to pretend it wasn't serious and everything would be back to normal very soon. Consequently I made no changes to my lifestyle. This was a defining moment for me. I leaned over to my bedside table and pulled out a notebook and pen; proceeding to jot down what was preventing me from embracing life and how I needed to start the ball rolling for change. I still have that list.

Everything was mainly down to the exhaustion. I knew I had to make changes. I began my journey. Looking at the list, I needed to make some quick wins, so addressed each point immediately

1. Exhaustion – new earlier bedtime routine – have blood test for vitamin deficiency (the blood test discovered I was dangerously low in vitamin d and needed to take 1000 units per day for life. No wonder I was knackered)
2. Side effects from my medication – research all brands and their most common side effects – read reviews – decide which brand I was going to take and stick to it.
3. Unorganised because of number 1 – make to do list
4. Uninterested in anything or anyone because of number 1 – ring all my friends and arrange a catch up
5. Struggling with my thoughts – not with my experience, but with guilt and the recent loss of my sister – make a plan for self-therapy - write a book and get it all out of my system.

Even though being mindful was not a new concept for me, this was the second I began to take back control and be self-aware.

I wrote and self-published my first book "A True Story of Love, Loss and Survival – 4 sisters battle cancer" It was a means of release, enabling me to let go of past experiences that were holding me back. Your life experiences are not just memories; they govern how you respond to situations and the choices you make today. There is some research from Southern Methodist University which states "if you write about your difficult life experiences then it would show improvement to your physical and mental health". It builds your strength and allows you to deal with difficulties in your life. A nightmare of thoughts was locked in my memory. Somewhere in a box in the depth of my recall bursting to get out and be set free. My book allowed this to happen. It enabled me to breathe again.

After all I went through in book 1; book 2 is where the journey to happiness had to begin. I will never forget but I will not let the past define my happiness today. Now I am ready to share with you some techniques that will enable you to have a beautiful life. Before you can make any changes, you must be mindful and self-aware, so this is OUR beginning. It is incredibly significant in all areas of our lives. Self-awareness will allow you to recognise zones that need improvement before they become problematic. It is recognising your strengths, weaknesses, your emotions at any given time. It is having a clear perception of your personality traits, your thoughts, beliefs and what drives you. Someone who is self-aware understands others and how they are perceived.

Who originally came up with the idea of self-awareness? It was first made a theory in 1972 by Duval and Wicklund in their book 'A Theory of Objective Self-Awareness'.

There are many rich and famous people who are desperately unhappy. Life is about being at peace with yourself, accepting who you are and loving who you are. It is being kind yet assertive to others, accepting and fulfilling your responsibilities. Putting

100% effort into your work, people who are important to you and filling your spare time with what makes you happy. These are just a few things that are important to me and are, in my opinion, areas that you need to be aware of. If one or more of these areas are not in sync then it could have an effect on your wellbeing. However, unless you are self-aware it may become unnoticed and unaddressed which could lead to unhappiness.

It will be your most powerful weapon and will get you where you want to be in life as long as you know how to use it to your advantage. Should you be asked in an interview what your greatest strength is, an answer that would be a game changer is "self-awareness".

You may be feel that you are already aware of your emotions, but to what scale? Think about it – think about the last time you reacted to a situation based on your emotions and regretted it later, instead of being proactive and responding based on the practicalities of the situation. 'Guilty!' My daughter will vouch for that! But I am getting better; I am tuned in to my weakness. Each time I feel a reaction on the horizon, I take a step back and count to ten. It does not mean you are a push over, quite the opposite. It shows strength of character to stay calm and respond in a more controlled state.

Life is all about continuous self-development. My journey began with copious amounts of research, leading me to numerous helpful therapies. I have simplified the ones that worked for me and I am confident they will work for you too.

This is the first step to taking control of your life and creating what you want. You will be able to recognise where your thoughts and emotions are taking you and divert to a more engaging level.

I am sure the majority of you reading this have reached a crossroads in your life more than once. Am I right? Imagine yourself at that crossroads now where you are not sure which path to take – there are so many questions to answer before you can make that decision. Maybe you have been hit with one challenge after another. Each time you pull yourself up to fight another day, something else knocks you down or it could be you have reached a stage in your life where you know you need to make changes but where do you start. Well you start right here!

You will not change just by reading this. It is something you have to practice, something you have to physically do. You may see aspects of your behaviour you didn't notice before. Think of it like learning to drive. You cannot physically learn to drive by reading about it. You have to practice it. You have to be aware of what your feet are doing whilst observing what is going on around you, whilst listening to instructions. Learning to be self-aware is similar. It is stopping in the moment and thinking about your emotions, reactions, strengths, weaknesses. It is allowing you to pause before reacting to circumstances, or statements from others. It is paying attention to your own personality, emotions and beliefs. Once you are able to master this then you will quickly recognise traits of others which will allow you to build more solid relationships and manage any that need attention. Believe me if you allow yourself to become self-aware, you are opening yourself up to a whole new world. Life begins at the edge of your comfort zone!

I achieved my short term goals i.e. the list – now it was time to begin my journey and create long term change. Here is how I did it.

# Tip 1 – What are your Drivers and Values?

I began by looking at my values - what motivated me to get up in the morning?

I sensed that if I had a better understanding of myself, I would come to realise how unique I am as an individual and what is in my heart is exclusive to me. I would have the thinking capability to judge my own performance and respond appropriately to different situations.

Taking time to think about and listen to what I value in life was an important step. I suggest you do the same - What energises you and motivates you to feel like you are achieving? What motivates you to feel you are a good person and of value? Unless you know what makes you sad, you cannot change it and unless you know what makes you happy, you cannot nurture it. If you feel your partner, family, friend or colleague is contributing to your unhappiness, what are they are doing or saying that is causing you to feel low? Is it something you could discuss and bring to their attention as to how they are making you feel? Could you change your approach to them to create a better outcome?

---

Let me bring you forward a year; December 26th 2018. I haven't done much writing at all for quite a few months. I often procrastinate. If I unintentionally break the habit, it is months before my fingers touch the keyboard.

Even though the past six months have passed in the blink of an eye, they have been some of the most emotionally challenging months for a long time. My husband is ill at the moment which has been particularly complicated and extremely worrying. My daughter and I have not been on good terms over Christmas. I was made redundant from my job, however after gruelling assessment centres I have managed to secure an equally challenging role. So let's say this Christmas has been one of the worst, the first Christmas ever in my life without a Christmas tree. I have taken this opportunity to spend it relaxing and planning the changes I am going to make in 2019. This is going to be my year! And yours!

What are *your* values in life? What would *you* like to work on? Initially you may start out thinking of the superficial things that matter to you like taking a holiday in your fantasy place or making a massive purchase on your dream car. These things can lose their lustre very quickly. Take a step back for a moment and look at what is REALLY important to you, what you would like to achieve and what makes you happy.

Being aware of my values in life enabled me to focus on the areas for change. Try not to focus on what is going to get in the way because you will create that problem to happen. Why? Because our unconscious mind has no control, it will only think, behave or produce the mood that our conscious mind feeds it. You can programme your mind to be in a positive mood – Yes, you really are in that much control. According to Agnes, when we talk to ourselves about our focus, goals OR the things that are going to hold us back, the information enters our filters and we can see the pictures and hear the sounds. They are representations of reality, not reality itself.

Instead of thinking how difficult something is, think about what you will get out of it. For example, rather than thinking about how you can't be bothered, focus on how good you will feel when you have done it.

I was not sure what my values were or how to prioritise them, so I proceeded to draw a circle like the one below and divided it up into sections – I then scored each section in order of its priority in my world, putting a cross on each line as to how relevant it was to me. The outside scoring 10 and the inside scoring 0. Joining up the crosses gave me the shape of my wheel. I have put some examples in the circle below but you can fill the sections with your own personal values. Don't forget to score each one from 0 to 10. Would your wheel travel smoothly on the ground? According to Lindsey Agnes (Change your life with NLP), all these areas need to be in balance to achieve harmony and success. If one or more are out of balance we are more likely to suffer from stress. (Next book "say yes to no stress")

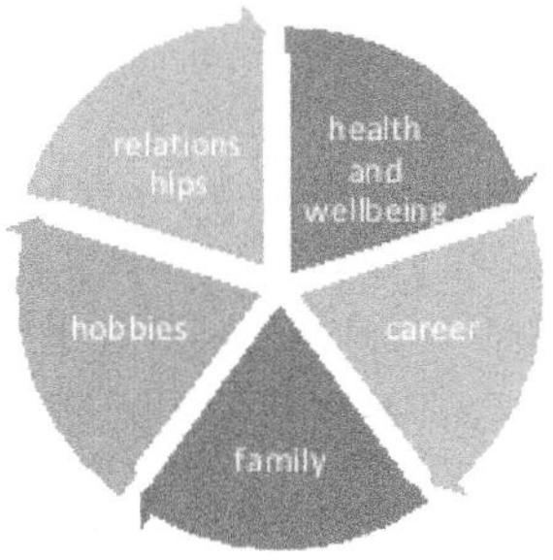


Once I became aware of what was going on in my world I could begin to challenge and change my old beliefs. Focus your energy on what excites you!!!

Eighteen months ago when I found myself exhausted and vulnerable, I had a light bulb moment when I suddenly realised it was time for me to take control. To give myself what I deserved, a happy life. That is all – a happy life. I knew there was no way I could achieve this unless changes took place. I became aware of my emotions, my values and beliefs. Some I wanted to keep, some I wanted to change but it was my decision and I was in control.

Author Thomas Bien declares "every moment can be a moment of happiness if you concentrate hard enough" Practice tuning into your senses, smelling the coffee you are sipping, tasting the food you are eating. Focus on what your body is feeling to maximise the moment. Don't chase something because you think you should or because it makes someone else happy so it will work for you – it won't. Search your heart and soul for what makes you feel warm inside. Success and happiness is at your fingertips. It could be sitting with a glass of wine and a good book, spending quality time with your family or focusing on changing your job and finding one that energises you. Whatever it is keep it simple!

# Tip 2 – Understand and accept your past experiences

"Accept your past without regret, handle your present with confidence and face your future without fear"

My next phase was to reflect on my early life story. People, events and experiences have had a massive impact in shaping the person I have become and the same applies to you. Think about it, accept it. We cannot change the past. There is no getting away from it – your past has helped to shape you. Anything you have experienced has had an impact on you – some massively and some slightly. I am not going to labour this one. It is what it is and you know what to do.

Being a parent has been the most difficult, exhausting, heart breaking, heart-warming, stressful, rewarding experience of my life. It has made me appreciate the fantastic way my own parents (who were not perfect) maintained a loving family full of warmth and acceptance in some very challenging circumstances. I was always challenging their tolerance. When I was twelve years old, I came home one day to inform them, quite categorically, I was going to be a Mormon. I had been spending time over the summer with my friend and her aunt (who was a Mormon) and yes, I had made my decision. It wasn't one of my finest moments let me tell ya! Given my parents were devote Irish Catholics. I think my father dropped to his knees to say the rosary! I am sure as I became a teenager they lived in fear of what the hell I was going to do next!

There is no drill or training school. Maybe it should be in the curriculum. We all make mistakes but we do the best we can. If your parents have made mistakes that have had an impact on you, try not to blame them. Try understand that they were doing what they thought was right (obviously within reason). You are an adult now and are responsible for how you deal with your past – you can change your thought patterns and shift your paradigm.

Writing about my past experiences helped me dramatically to accept the changes in me and my life. All the feelings and memories (not about my parents but experiences) that I was reluctant to recall and kept in a box in the back of my mind with the lid firmly closed were released, dealt with and accepted.

I was recently having an in depth discussion with a friend who has experienced cancer. Unfortunately it left her with irreversible disabilities (to look at her you wouldn't know anything was different). She explained to me how difficult it was to come to terms with these disabilities and the impact it has had on her life moving forward. She struggled desperately with the changes, this steered her in the direction of therapy. The outcome; she was grieving for her old life, who wouldn't be? However, it was something she could not influence and was holding her back from enjoying her present life and moving on. She couldn't believe the difference this made to her mental attitude. This is her life now and she accepts it. To be honest if you are reading this you will know it is about you and you look amazing! You are an inspiration.

You have no control over what has happened in the past but you have control over how you deal with it now. By holding on to past experiences, it places you in the unfortunate situation of reliving the pain over and over again. This is what my friend was experiencing. How can you bring joy and positivity into your life when it is filled up with pain and hurt? Make space for happiness by letting go of your past.

Understand you have a choice and make the decision to set it free. It is not easy and I am not saying it is. Think about your individual situation. You will not be able to move on until you accept your past. You cannot change it – believe me I know! I have accepted everything that has happened to me and realised my experiences have made me who I am today. It is not what has happened but how you deal with it. Believe me, at this moment in my life, Christmas 2018, I am experiencing challenges that I never expected would be presented to me in a lifetime let alone all together. Some days it has been essential to allow myself a meltdown. God knows I've earnt it. I get it out of my system and rise above it. I cannot let external forces drain me and prevent me from living MY life. I will help find a solution to the problem. I will be empathic, loving and caring. However to take on the responsibility of someone else's world is far too much to ask of anyone. There is no one responsible for MY world only me!

Like I said - this is the first Christmas in my entire life that I have not had a Christmas tree or any decorations. Bring on Christmas 2019 because boy am I going to celebrate!!

2019 is my year. I am going to achieve, be successful with my own goals, some very small and some quite ambitious. I am going to love and be loved and most of all I am going to smile from my heart.

Living in the past will slow you down. It doesn't matter how you have lived your life until this moment. All that matters is what your dreams are now. Now you make your own choices. Change can happen in the blink of an eye. So make that decision today. See your life as an adventure and you will start to enjoy the journey. Give yourself permission to be happy and welcome optimism back into your life.

Scepticism and negativity is a habit you have created at some point without realising it. You can break this bad habit and create a good habit of optimism and positivity. I truly accept and embrace who I am today. I feel deeply satisfied with my achievements over the years and my integrity as a person. I'm not perfect but I accept it. Generally I am a positive, confident woman which I can honestly say has been achieved through habitual thoughts. Once you become aware of the fact that changing your habits can transform your life, you will be on the road to improving your world on so many levels. Here's how.

# Tip 3 Make a decision and create new habits

We all want to make changes for the better. Within my social group of friends, we talk about nothing else! We want it to be simple without any effort, but it's not. We are all of the opinion that change is daunting. The first step to making it easy is to know what you want to change.

What *is* change? It is breaking the cycle, an addiction we have created due to a conditioned way of thinking.

At the beginning of this book I explained to you my physical and spiritual self were not in tune, therefore I was looking to make alterations and more importantly be self-aware and recognise exactly WHAT I desired to alter.

I began to research change and discovered we have on average 60,000 thoughts a day. Surprisingly 95% of these thoughts are the same as we had the day before, proving we are a product of our own habits.

Research has shown that by the age of 35 we have developed a personality set by memorised behaviours, emotional reactions, unconscious attitudes and beliefs that operate on a sub-conscious level. We are driven by a set of habits which have been set through repetition. I am a firm believer that the way we live, our actions, thoughts, behaviours are a product of habits we have created, consciously and sub-consciously.

I soon realised in order to make improvements I needed to develop the ability to change my habits, recognising this would give me so much power to control my life. A very simple example would be about three months ago I had my six monthly check-up at the dentist. She told me I had mild to moderate gum disease due to missing certain areas around my gums when brushing. Personally I thought my brushing routine was up there, but obviously not. I was advised to be more thorough and to use the interdental brushes (*as she had advised me six months previous!*) How long does it take? 1 minute? But it really was an effort. I had to place the little brush next to my toothbrush to remind me and it didn't take long before it became a firm habit. I even take one out with me and floss in the car whilst driving. Our life is made up of habits from birth – being potty trained, bedtime routine. I began to get excited with the thought of how this simple theory could change my entire life.

When we have a thought, our brain creates chemicals associated with that thought – this is our emotion. According to research, our bodies crave the emotional chemicals. When we try to change we become very uncomfortable. The chemical balance is not the norm and our bodies strive for what is familiar. This is when we hear the negative voices telling us to "start tomorrow" or "this is too difficult" Hence the reason it is so challenging.

According to the experts, it takes about 21 days to break or form a habit of medium difficulty. Habits which are more difficult may take longer. Three weeks may not sound like a very long time, but you can create powerful habits within 21 days. Such as getting up earlier at a specific hour, going running in the morning, cycling, going to bed at a certain time, having a daily facial beauty routine, a daily exercise routine or being punctual for appointments. These are the medium difficulty habits that can be quite easily developed in 14-21 days through practice and repetition.

According to Brian Tracey, over the years, a simple, powerful, proven methodology has been determined for new habit development. It is very much like a recipe for preparing a dish in the kitchen. You can use it to develop any habit that you desire. Over time, you will find it easier and easier to develop the habits that you want to incorporate into your personality. He goes on to say the time period to create a habit can be any length from a single second to several years. The speed of new habit pattern development is largely determined by *the intensity of the emotion* that accompanies the decision to begin acting in a particular way.

Every New Year I decide to adopt a healthier lifestyle and usually by week two, old habits creep in and I am back to square one, reaching for the chocolate due to boredom or just because I bloody love it! But what if the doctor told me "lose a stone or you will die at an early age" now that would certainly whip me into shape?

Suddenly, the thought of dying would be so scary that I would make immediate changes to become healthier. Psychologists refer to this as a *"significant emotional experience."* Any experience of intense joy or pain, combined with behaviour, can create a habitual behaviour pattern that may be sustained for the rest of a person's life.

For example, putting your hand on a hot stove or touching a live electrical wire will give you an intense and immediate pain or shock. The experience may only take a split second. But for the rest of your life, you will have developed the habit of not putting your hand on hot stoves, or touching live electrical wires. The habit will have been formed instantly and permanently.

Here are the recommended steps to help you create a habit;

1) Make a decision

First, make a decision. Decide clearly that you are going to begin acting in a specific way 100% of the time, whenever that behaviour is required. For example, if you decide to rise early and exercise each morning, set your clock for a specific time, and when the alarm goes off, immediately get up, put on your exercise clothes and begin your exercise session.

2) Never allow an exception to your new habit

Second, never allow an exception to your new habit during the formative stages. Don't make excuses or rationalisations. Don't let yourself off the hook. If you desire to get up at 6:00am each morning, discipline yourself to get up at 6:00am, every single morning until this becomes automatic.

3) Tell others you are practicing a new behaviour

Third, tell others that you are going to begin practicing a particular behaviour. It is amazing how much more disciplined and determined you will become when you know that others are watching you to see if you have the willpower to follow through on your resolution.

4) Visualize your new habit

Fourth, visualize yourself performing or behaving in a particular way in a particular situation. The more often you visualize and imagine yourself acting as if you already had the new habit, the more rapidly this new behaviour will be accepted by your subconscious mind and become automatic.

5) Create an affirmation

Fifth, create an affirmation that you repeat over and over to yourself. This repetition dramatically increases the speed at which you develop the new habit. For example, you can say something like, *"I get up and get going immediately at 6:00am each morning!"* Repeat these words the last thing before you fall asleep. In most cases, you will automatically wake up minutes before the alarm clock goes off, and soon you will need no alarm clock at all.

6) Resolve to persist

Sixth, persist in the new behaviour until it is so automatic and easy that you actually feel uncomfortable when you do not do what you have decided to do.

7) Reward yourself

Seventh, and most important, give yourself a reward of some kind for practicing the new behaviour. Each time you reward yourself; you reaffirm and reinforce the behaviour. Soon you begin to associate, at an unconscious level, the pleasure of the reward with the behaviour. You set up your own force field of positive consequences that you unconsciously look forward to as the result of engaging in the behaviour or habit that you have decided upon.

I have put these steps into practice. I wouldn't dream of asking you to do something I haven't done myself.

I am such a procrastinator when it comes to my writing, a sure sign of a perfectionist. I put it off even though it is something that relaxes me and provides me with a sense of achievement. So my habit was to spend at least 1 hour per day writing, either working on my webpage or my next book. In the past I have balanced my laptop on my knee whilst watching TV. Isn't it just so uncomfortable? So I decided to prepare myself an area in the house for me to write. I made it inviting, tidy and organised. I plan it into my diary with my work commitments. In the evening I light some scented candles and take up a large glass of wine. Boy does that do the trick! I literally can't wait to get up there. So the steps work as long as the habit is something you are committed to. My aim was to focus on the goal and why I wanted it.

Don't judge yourself if you slip up - for example;

"I had one piece of cake and ruined my diet so I may as well eat the lot"

"I haven't sat down to write for a week so what is the point"

"I have put 2 pounds on so I may as well forget it"

My most common mistake is "If it isn't perfect it isn't worth it!

- This is so the wrong attitude. In the infancy of practicing your habit, be strict without tweaking but if you make a mistake don't give up.

Your next challenge is to make sure any changes will stick!

Why do we sometimes slip back into old habits? You need clarity on your reasons why you are doing this. For example "the reason I want to become healthier is because I am frequently out of breath when walking" Habit; Walk 2 miles every morning.

Practice Practice Practice; if possible around the same time each day. Practice, reflect, and create triggers to remind you.

Successful change begins with clarity and purpose and ends with discipline and practice.

# Tip 4 – Create a daily habit of being Self-aware

Next I decided to develop a daily practice of setting aside at least twenty minutes to reflect. This practice allowed me to focus on the things that are important to me. What was creating happiness or sadness in my world? How was I feeling about it? Most definitely there is a direct correlation between mindfulness and changes in the brain – moving you away from anger and anxiety and toward a sense of calm and well-being.

Reflection can take many forms. Keeping a journal, meditation or just simply taking a long walk adding serenity to your existence. My handsome ginger pooch whiskey has become solely my responsibility. I knew he would, years ago on that misty evening when we were "only looking" at pups. I was bombarded with emotional pressure and the promises of duty, not only from my children, but my husband too. "We will walk him constantly, play with him, feed him, teach him to read" You get the picture? Well 8 years later; the kids have left home and have their own families, my husband has pressure sores from being educated by "come dine with me" and I find myself walking Whiskey morning and evening, an hour each time and when my demanding job dictates me not fitting walkies into my hectic schedule, I pay my ever dependable walker to assist.

There are many mornings and evenings when the rain is lashing down and being drenched feels far from serene but once out there I utilise the time. Whiskey is receiving his walk and I am power walking, being mindful, thinking about my day, what I would like to achieve or listening to my favourite music. I use it as an excuse to socialise with friends, walking the dogs together, sometimes calling in the local pub for a glass of wine. All these activities are achieved whilst walking my dog.

Indian researchers found that undergraduate students with higher mindfulness had greater resilience and life satisfaction.

Mindful people can better cope with difficult thoughts and emotions without becoming overwhelmed or shutting down. Let me simplify this by repeating – mindfulness is focusing on your emotions, thoughts, sensations, so you can be aware of them without actually labelling them. Thoughts are not facts and by being mindful you can prevent them from becoming a deep rooted issue. This puts you in control for making better decisions in your life.

My life is very busy and bursting with demands of family, work, friends, hobbies etc. I wouldn't have it any other way. However, the days, weeks, months have a tendency to evaporate into thin air and the only way to slow it down is to be self-ware and mindful. It is a habit of mine and something I do, constantly if I am being honest. It just happens naturally because I have done it for so long. It allows me to appreciate the life I have. It also prevents me from procrastinating – I know what I want to do and most of the time I just get on and do it.

What are *your* thoughts, emotions, words, behaviour right now – unless you know this you cannot make changes. Mindfulness is such a buzz word at the moment. What do I hear you saying? You don't have time to think about what is happening now because you are too busy thinking about what needs doing tomorrow. This is the problem. We need to slow it down. I am not saying don't think about the past or the future. It is having the ability to go back and forth and not getting stuck in the past or dwelling. It would be unrealistic to say just think of NOW. It is about having a more helpful relationship with your thinking. True mindfulness is about knowing where you are right now (being in the moment) but also having an awareness of – but not getting stuck in – where you have been (reflection) and where you are going (anticipating). *Gill Hasson bestselling author of Mindfulness and Emotional Intelligence.*

How is being mindful helpful? In my opinion, like I have just mentioned, the world is so fast and stressful. Sometimes having demands, deadlines and commitments often enables time to pass too quickly for me to have appreciation. Mindfulness permits me to appreciate my experiences instead of rushing through life constantly trying to be somewhere else. There are many ways of practicing mindfulness. I could go on forever but this is an overview. If you need techniques and ideas you can google for suggestions to inspire you.

# Tip 5 – Be proactive not reactive

Have you ever had an argument with someone who has said such hurtful comments that they couldn't possibly be in control of their emotions? I certainly have and I have to be honest at times I react back on my emotions too. This is what motivated me to research this and become more proactive in my approach. The reactive people in question are so unaware of how their actions and words affect me. It really hurts me, not just the words because to be honest I am pretty thick skinned. I have enough confidence in myself to not let words affect my self-belief. It is the lack of respect for me, the fact someone feels it is ok to cross that boundary.

Like I said, I am not entirely innocent as I can respond back based on my emotions too, fuelling the situation further encouraging a disturbing outcome. Somehow my mind-set had developed an irresponsible thought pattern, telling me it would show weakness not to mirror this behaviour. This could not be further from the truth. It displays such strength to take a step back and think logically about the situation. It takes strength to respond in a non-aggressive manner.

My aim is to set boundaries for myself and others. There is a line that must not be crossed. My gut feeling is my trusted friend and I will always know when I am on the right track. If I feel someone is being unkind to me, I need to recognise it instantly and change my behaviour.

I would like you to think about how you react to situations. You could quite categorically enhance your quality of life by being aware of your reactions and making some changes.

This section is all about responsibility and control, about taking a pause for a couple of seconds in order to think about your response. My aim was to create healthier relationships.

Habit 1 – Be Proactive; from the worldwide popular book "The 7 Habits of Highly Effective People by Stephen Covey" This is about taking responsibility for your life. You **cannot** constantly keep finding someone or something to blame for your actions or behaviour. **Proactive** people accept but don't blame genetics, circumstances or conditions for the way things have turned out for them. They know only too well that they have a choice to make changes.

I soon realised, genetics, circumstances and conditions are external forces and act as stimuli that we respond to. Between the stimulus and the response is where we are in control – we have the freedom to choose our response. One of the most important things we choose is what we say. The way we speak in terms of choice of words and tone is a good indicator of how we see ourselves and how others perceive us. A proactive person uses proactive language–I can, I will, I prefer, etc. A reactive person uses reactive language–I can't, I have to, if only. Reactive people feel they have no choice.

Proactive people put their emphasis on their Circle of Influence. They work on the things they can do something about: weight, general health, problems at work, education etc.

Reactive people focus their efforts in the Circle of Concern–things over which they have little or no control: the national debt, terrorism, the weather, age etc. It is safe to say the majority of us are not aware of what is consuming our energy, me included. It has taken a lot of time and focus for me to realise what is in my circle of influence and my circle of concern and although it has not been easy, instead of panicking about getting older, I am beginning to embrace what getting older brings to my life. Of course it goes without saying if someone could wave a magic wand, I would give up my right arm to shave 20 years off but that is never going to happen so why wish for it. 50 is the new 30 and I still take great pride in myself – end of! What if I was 70 and had been granted a wish to go back 20 years. Well – here I am jumping for joy. What I am really saying is; I cannot do anything about my age but I can do something about how I take care of myself and my appearance. I cannot do anything about reaching retirement but I can enjoy my life now and prepare to enjoy my retirement. I love to write and so my intentions are to continue developing my writing skills which will serve me when I have more time on my hands.

Becoming aware of the areas we are focusing on that consume our energies without positive results is a giant step in becoming proactive.

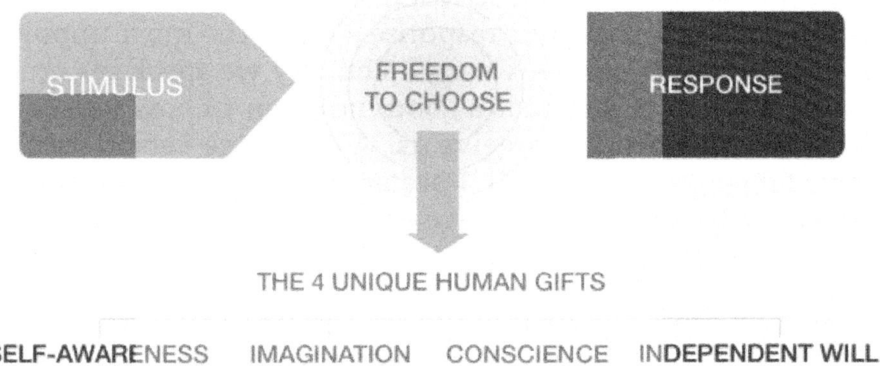


A **proactive** swimmer anticipates that there will be waves, whereas the **reactive** one is painfully surprised by each wave. ... So, being **proactive** means being able to anticipate what the future will be and to react accordingly before it actually happens.

Do you consider yourself proactive or reactive?

How can you be proactive instead of reactive?

What does it mean to be "proactive", as opposed to "reactive"? And how can you do it?

When you are being reactive, you are not taking initiative. You let the events control your response. You're thrown into turmoil by the tides of life. Each new wave catches you by surprise. It takes an enormous amount of energy for you scramble to react to it in order to just stay afloat.

Going back to the swimmer anticipating the waves, let's say *you're* in choppy waters and you are proactive. It's not just that you anticipate the waves. You're in tune with them. You're not desperately trying to escape them; you're dancing with them.

It would be great to dance with the rhythm of life but is this only possible to those people who are endowed with a proactive attitude (or, maybe, a "proactive gene")?

In a nutshell, being proactive is the same thing as being reactive. The only difference is: you do the reacting ahead of time.

So, being proactive means being able to anticipate what the future will be and to react accordingly before it actually happens.

What is it that prevents the reactive swimmer from doing so? It could be lack of information. There are plenty of events in life that we simply cannot predict. It could also be lack of intelligence: some people are better than others at thinking in terms of patterns.

But let's assume, for the moment, that our two swimmers have both the same levels of information and intelligence. Then, the difference between them would simply be that the proactive swimmer has enough energy to take in the available information and adapt to it. In contrast, the reactive swimmer is exhausted and overwhelmed

Some text adapted from (*"Somebody get me out of here, please!"*)

How can we react in a more positive way to situations?

ONE: To be proactive, what you have to do is ask yourself what is likely to happen, and react to it before it happens.

TWO: It takes energy to rise above the difficulties of the moment, to see the big picture and make the changes you need to make.

THREE: Sometimes, you may not have that energy. Don't think of yourself as being weak at these times. Think of your "reactivity" as a symptom instead of a failure. You need a break. Take it.

Sometimes taking a step back and evaluating the situation will allow you to refocus and change your approach.

Stephen Covey – Habit 1*: Be Proactive Synopsis*

"People are just about as happy as they make up their mind to be." – Abraham Lincoln

Every day you and I have a choice – to be happy or to be sad. People don't make you do things. You are in control. Take responsibility for your life.

We can only control one thing; we can control our reaction to what happens to us. We cannot control all actions but we can control our reactions.

Take responsibility for everything in your life and make choices based upon your values.

Proactive people don't worry about things they cannot influence. They are resilient and continue to bounce back having a "can-do" attitude.

Reactive people make choices based on impulse, continually blaming others – being a victim.

Don't be a victim. Stay away from the "Victimitis Virus" – a feeling that you are doomed. The world does not owe you a favour! Reactive people get angry and aggressive saying regretful things in the moment. They will only make changes when they are forced to.

## Reactive and Proactive language

Listen to the language. You can hear the difference between proactive (positive) and reactive (negative) people.

Proactive language puts you in control.

Before you react push the pause button and think about how you want to respond. This is not easy to do; this is challenging for me as my default is to react with impulse. I tend to constantly buzz about getting things done; should a bright idea come to mind, I need to act fast, yesterday, for fear of forgetting or missing some key fact. I am aware of this and working on slowing down my thought patterns, which is the motivation behind why I have included this tip - for you!

**Examples of Proactive and Reactive language**

| Reactive Language | Proactive Language |
|---|---|
| I'll try | I'll do it |
| There's nothing I can do | let's look at our options |
| I can't | There's got to be a way |

**Examples of Proactive and Reactive behaviours**

| Reactive behaviour | Proactive behaviour |
|---|---|
| Complain about situations | Make Changes to situations |
| Easily offended | not easily offended |
| Whine and complain | Bounce back |
| Wait for things to happen | Always find ways to make it happen |

**Circle of Control**

We are not in control of everything that happens to us – fact.

What we CAN control is how we respond to what happens to us.

Stop worrying about things you can't control and start worrying about things you can.

Imagine two circles. The inner circle is the circle of control. These are things you have control over (your attitude, yourself, your choices, your responses).

The outside circle is the circle of no control. These are things you have no control over. It has about a thousand things in it that you can't do anything about (your race, weather, rude comments, etc.)

Your Circle of Control is much smaller than the Circle of No Control.

Don't waste time waiting for your external to change and don't spend time and energy trying to change things that you have no control over.

Proactive people learn to live with things they can't do anything about and focus on things they can influence. By doing so they are in greater control of their lives and are more at peace.

# Tip 6 – Can being self-aware make you thin?

Amongst my research and discussions with friends about being self-aware, one of the questions that popped up was "could being self-aware make me lose weight quicker and keep it off?" Pardon the pun but the comment gave me food for thought. One of my changes was to look and feel healthier.

So the question is, how much do your thoughts contribute to your weight? Is weight all a matter of calories in/calories out, or are there other aspects to consider?

We are all chasing the perfect body – guilty!! And by that I don't necessarily mean thin. Perfect to me will not match perfect to you. Perfect is what you feel comfortable and confident with. I chose the title for this section based on the fact that personally I wanted to feel healthier with more energy and yes, I wanted to shed a few pounds, so shoot me. I know what you are saying, is it politically correct to say thin or fat? But I am being honest and I apologise if I offend anyone in the process.

I believe you can think yourself thin as much as you can think yourself fat. Which of these comments do you think would contribute to you being thin or fat?

"I will always be fat"

"I have had a biscuit I may as well have the whole packet"

"I desire food more than I desire to be thin"

"I have had a pizza but that will not stop me being healthy moving forward"

"I can be healthy I just have to make better choices and commit to it"

I will say one word - Metabolism – who the f... gave me a slow one??? Anyway I digress!

You have to decide first WHY? What is your motivation and constantly keep this in mind. Is it to be thinner? Look more attractive, younger and fitter? Fit in with your social group? Be accepted OR be healthier? Have more energy – physically and mentally? Live longer? Spring out of bed in the morning with a love for yourself and life? What energises you? You need to look deep within yourself and find that energy for life.

My "why" will be totally different to yours. It is personal to me but I will share it with you just to give you some idea of what you need to dig for within yourself. I have been given the most precious gift of life. To some of you that will sound lame, dramatic, boring but to others and you know who you are, it will resonate profoundly. I have lost 2 of my sisters to Cancer and my remaining sister survived like myself. I was with them when they took their last breath. So I want, need and have a burning desire to embrace the time I have on this earth. Yes I want to look the best I can look, but most of all I want to feel the energy for life and reward my body for being strong and experiencing the hurt and devastation cancer thrust upon it. I want to jump out of bed and embrace the day. By the end of the day the need to have achieved. Not to be crawling into bed exhausted, counting the hours in dread before I have to get up again.

Now let's be honest here, I am perplexed at the fact that without effort, I am self-aware in most areas of my life, it has become a habit. However when it comes to my food, self-awareness scarpers like a rat up a drainpipe. I can eat something unhealthy and afterwards I suddenly realise I forget to be self-aware. I forgot I wanted to make better choices! It's so annoying ☺ yet – I don't give up. I keep trying and that's the key.

So – where were we? You need to list your reasons why.

Don't make it complicated because it really isn't – Keep it simple. I wrote a checklist of my reasons, with the most important at the top. There will definitely be similarities in all our lists but the differences will be the order of importance.

1. Have a healthy body and mind
2. Get out of the bed every morning at 6am with zest
3. Have more energy to fulfil each day with something enjoyable (My family - grandchild, socialising with my sister and friends, my support group, writing, job, exercising)
4. Look Fitter, more attractive, thinner, the list goes on
5. Feel great in my clothes

The quality of the calories we eat are so essential to a healthy weight loss.

What I am trying to say here is when we gain weight we tend to cut down on our calories. What we should be doing is selecting healthier foods, being creative with them to make them tasty to eat. The worse choice you could make is reach for low calorie, pre packed food. Healthy wholesome foods inhibit appetite and increase energy whilst processed foods increase hunger and fat storage.

Dr David Ludwig, author of "always hungry" declared that when we put on weight something has triggered the fat cells to store too much energy. Some of these triggers are refined grains, starches and sugars found in many low calorie foods. He goes on to say that excess insulin secretion causes cells to retain fat rather than using it to fuel the body. 10 or 20 calories stored as excess fat each day can lead to obesity over the years.

Foods that are higher in calories like meat and dairy foods will nourish your body when eaten in a balanced way. Natural foods like veg do not need labels. The thing is not to count calories but to understand your eating habits and make good choices MOST of the time. You don't need to restrict your calories – what I have discovered by researching is that I can undo decades of unbalanced and excessive eating by sticking to a variety of high quality fresh, natural, unprocessed foods. If it helps you, keep a journal in your kitchen drawer to jot down what you eat. This will give you an idea if you are on the right track. BUT please do not get obsessed with it. ENJOY YOUR FOOD. There is constant information being fed into our unconscious minds about certain diets and what is good for you to eat etc. but these companies make millions from us and we are lining their pockets whilst at the same time gaining weight with constant fatigue and hating ourselves for it.

To the minority of sisters out there who are thin and need to gain a few pounds – go on a diet! You will gain weight I promise you, it's guaranteed.

Let's keep it simple – if we want to be healthy we need to eat the right foods in the right combinations at the right time.

Your struggle with weight is not completely your fault. We listen to the advice from marketing companies who are desperate to make money and tell us what we want to hear about weight loss strategies and packaged foods. Believe me they don't work long term or we would all be thin and healthy. As soon as you lose the weight and gradually start eating normal the weight piles back on with interest.

Try to observe slim, healthy people eating in a restaurant. Not all the time but generally they have made healthy choices and are eating slowly. They have created good habits of choosing foods that taste good and have a value to their body. They are choosing food from a different place in their minds by being aware.

You will be pleased to know eating healthy is not about eating health bars and carrot sticks. If you eat the right carbs with the right amount of protein the fat will burn off naturally

Irene Rubaum-Keller is a psychotherapist who specialises in weight control. She believes our weight is a combination of our genes, our thoughts, our feelings and our behaviours.

Our thoughts, feelings and behaviours are things we can control, where our genes we cannot (remember the circle of control)

So do you think you can use your thoughts to help you lose weight?

“I can never lose weight.”

“I’ve tried every diet and nothing works for me.”

“I’ve always been fat, I’ll always be fat.”

“I start out great but then lose my motivation and stop.”

“Oh well, I’ve blown it so I’ll start again on Monday (when it’s Tuesday)”

If you have thoughts like the above then the answer is “NO – thoughts like the above will not help you lose weight.

Self-awareness is the key to long-term weight loss and weight maintenance. That means paying close attention to what we think, what we put into our bodies and how we feel. If these thoughts are below the conscious level, then we can do nothing to change them. We need to be aware of them first.

So the next step, once you have the awareness is to bust yourself. The thought police need to come in, guns drawn, and arrest those nasty, self-defeating thoughts.

Then, and most importantly, those thoughts need to be replaced with thoughts that will help you reach your goal. This works with any goal you are trying to achieve, not just weight control.

Some helpful replacement thoughts might be;

“Is that a choice that will move me in the direction I want to go?”

“I can reach my weight-loss goal.”

“I am successful and will continue to be.”

“My weight is in my control.”

“I can do this.”

I began to realise, Just as I need to change my eating habits to lose weight and keep it off, I need to change my thought habits as well. They go together. If I can get control of my self-defeating thoughts, I will have a much easier time controlling my behaviour and ultimately reaching my goal of a healthier lifestyle.

Can you think yourself thin? No not really, but you can think yourself to the behaviours that will make you thin. You can do this. It is in your control. - *Irene Rubaum-Keller*

Create for yourself a different lifestyle approach that doesn't require drastic dieting. I am sure you don't need me to tell you that the roller coaster of crash dieting is a one way ticket to fatigue, low self-esteem and extreme hunger. Give your body the best chance of being healthy.

Let's get one thing straight here, I have been every size invented by man, fat, thin and everything in-between. From about 18 – 40 I was generally slim. Some of it attractively slim and some not so attractively thin. For many years from being seventeen I was a sufferer of Anorexia and Bulimia (I plan to write a book about this) they were tough years, not just for me but for my parents and siblings. Yes I was very thin but the price was misery, decent and eventually an overdose. I set up and facilitated various support groups in my 20s and then again late 30s. I was reactive for many years blaming my parents when in actual fact it was my choice fuelled by vanity and a reinforced bad habit. I am not saying this is the case for everyone who has embarked on that journey but for me, I take responsibility.

3 simple tips to unlock the thin you

1. Be self-aware when eating and making choices
2. Commit and know your why? When choosing food get into the habit of thinking why you are wanting to be healthy
3. Break old habits and make new ones.

# Tip 7 – Know your colours and the colours of people around you

In 2017 for my career development, I was lucky enough to have a personal coach to nurture my skills in Emotional Intelligence. He would accompany me probably twice a month, when he would spend the day tutoring me how to use various aspects of emotional intelligence in order to build better relationships professionally and personally. The whole field force were being coached not just me. However, I was one of the few who embraced it and used it to my advantage. I am sure this is down to my background in psychology and the fact I am already bought into the theory.

I used Emotional Intelligence, amongst other things to help me achieve elite performer 2018 at the pharmaceutical company I currently work for and in one of my up and coming books "Basic tips for successful selling" will be a chapter on this in more detail.

I have concluded with personality profiling because it has a direct link to being mindful and self-aware and personally and professionally it will enable you to understand people close to you and in business. For example someone who is strong willed, has ambition and energy would suggest they are a RED. Someone who has a tendency to have a fixed set of principles and a desire to live according to these principles would suggest they are a BLUE.

How does this link into being self-aware? Should you have an understanding of what the personality traits are of others then you can adapt your actions and reactions in order to get the best out of your interactions.

What I have found in a sales situation, I have observed the surroundings of my customer in order to give myself an idea as to what colour they are likely to be. For example when I enter a consultant's office for an appointment, I will quickly check out the layout of the room. Is it neat and tidy, book shelves full of books, trial papers on his desk? Is he dressed very professional, suit and tie? I would immediately and automatically make a decision that he/she has a tendency to be BLUE. This would tell me he/she was analytical, facts and trial statistics would drive this customer's decision to prescribe. I know they would be irritated if I tried to sell on patient pictures and feelings so I would give them the trial statistics and outcomes that would show they are doing the job they spent years training for. One thing I can be sure of is if I can get this customer to agree to use my product, they will stick to their promise.

I am such a great believer in this theory and have had measurable success in implementing it. Knowing your colours or social style and the colours (social style) of others is a fundamental part of being emotionally intelligent. The quality and success of your relationships would dramatically improve if you can adapt your communication style to that of the person you are trying to connect with.

The theory suggests our individual characteristics fit into one or two of the following colours BLUE analytical style, YELLOW expressive style, RED driving style or GREEN amiable style. We can display the characteristics of all the colours but we generally revert to type and have a tendency to clash with the opposite. If you are backed into a corner, it is common to switch to the opposite type. For example if a green, who is amiable and will avoid conflict, is backed into a corner with an aggressive situation, they will switch to being a red – aggressive, rude and abrupt. Vice versa – if a red is backed into a corner, they tend to become passive and lack conviction.

When you read the following social styles (colours), you will be able to recognise them in your friends, family or work colleagues. Do you get frustrated when you spend the time writing a lengthy text to someone, only to receive a "yes" or "no" in return? That someone is probably a "Blue" and requires the facts only – don't go around the houses. How frustrating is it though?

Here is a brief outline of the colour characteristics.

**BLUE -** Low responsive – low assertive.

BLUEs are analytical and information orientated. BLUEs can appear unsociable especially to GREENs and YELLOWs. They are problem solvers, liking structure with the ability to organise. They have a strong sense of duty and are no nonsense people – do not flower things up, get straight to the point.

They are very cautious at making decisions, asking questions about specific details. A consequence of this is that they are persistent. However, once they have made their decision they stick to it and there is no wiggle room.

In a work environment they are task orientated and intellectual. They make good accountants or engineers.

A Blue would tend to be highly critical of people and pessimistic in nature but very perceptive.

**Characteristics:** Serious, mull matters over, indecisive, persistent; asks lots of questions, attention to detail.

**In conflict:** Whining, sarcastic, negative

**How to be with them:** Keep to the facts, don't agree with them and listen attentively

**Basic Need:** To be correct

**RED**

A RED person is a driver – low responsive – high assertiveness and objective focused.

They expect efficiency from everyone they come into contact with. They find it hard to build relationships and can be seen as aggressive and uncaring, especially by GREENs. They know what they want and how to get there. They communicate quickly and straight to the point but sometimes they are a little tackless. They can be an "ends justify the means" type of person. They are hard working with high energy and do not shy away from conflict and often will try to steam roller anyone who stands in their way.

**Characteristics:** Task orientated, clearly defined goals, committed, determined, risk taker, efficient.

**In conflict:** Aggressive, rude and abrupt

**How to be with them:** Be assertive and firm, have a solution to their problem, listen

**Basic Need:** To be in control

**YELLOW** High responsive – high assertive

A Yellow is an expressive person who is warm and enthusiastic. GREENs compliment them well unless the expressive becomes too aggressive and puts them off. They are good people to have at a party and interesting to be around. However if they don't get the attention they crave they can become difficult. The best way to deal with them in a conflict is to let them calm down and not to fuel the fire by saying anything controversial. They are natural salespeople or story tellers with good communication skills. They are excellent motivators but can be competitive and have a tendency to exaggerate, leaving out facts and details. Sometimes talking a lot about things rather than doing them.

**Characteristics:** People orientated, centre of attention, positive, emotional, talkative, enthusiastic, dramatic

**In conflict:** Unpredictable, emotional

**How to be with them:** Allow them to gain composure, ask questions, problem solve.

**Basic Need:** Recognition

**GREEN** High responsive – low assertive

Greens are amiable people who are kind hearted and avoid conflict. They are more of a listener than a talker – Yellows tend to like them because they are prepared to listen to what they are saying. They need to have a feeling of security so are unlikely to take risks. If pushed they are likely to make promises they cannot keep. Reds often find them frustrating because they want a straight answer and the GREENS can find this difficult to deliver. They can blend into any situation well. However, they can appear wishy washy and have difficulty making firm decisions. They often love art, music and poetry. They are highly sensitive, quiet and soft spoken

**Characteristics:** Loyal, personable, patient, uncomfortable with risk, non-confrontational, dislike pressure, enjoy the company of others

**In conflict:** Likely to be passive, lack conviction, avoidance

**How to be with them:** Reassure, support and confirm commitment

**Basic Need:** Security

# Conclusion "An Inspirational Teenager"

I would like to conclude with a poem by a teenager with cancer. I know it is a sad conclusion but I am sure the teenager would be immensely proud if it motivates you to be self-aware and appreciate the simple things in life that we only too well take for granted.

This poem was written by a terminally ill young girl in a New York hospital and passed on by her Consultant.

**The importance of being Self-aware – by a teenager with cancer**

.

**SLOW DANCE**

Have you ever watched kids on a merry-go-round?

Or listened to the rain slapping on the ground?

Ever followed a butterfly's erratic flight?

Or gazed at the sun into the fading light?

*You better slow down -Don't dance so fast - Time is short - The music won't last*

Do you run through each day on the fly?

When you ask "how are you?" do you hear the reply?

When the day is done do you lie in your bed?

With the next 100 chores running through your head?

*You better slow down -Don't dance so fast - Time is short - The music won't last*

Ever told your child we will do it tomorrow?

And in your haste not see his sorrow?

Ever lost touch, let a good friendship die?

Because you never had time to call and say Hi?

*You better slow down -Don't dance so fast - Time is short - The music won't last*

When you run so fast to get somewhere do you miss half the fun of getting there?

When you worry and hurry through your day, is it like and unopened gift just thrown away?

Life is not a race, do take it slower

Hear the music, before the song is over.

A real heart-warming message – Don't let time pass you by! Think about what you want to achieve and go get it.

Be self-aware and enjoy your life.

----

Please leave me a review

Do you have a question or comment? or would you like links to my other publications? you can email at pinkhammerton@gmail.com

Look out for my next book "Say Yes to NO STRESS"

amouraj.co.uk – Mission Self Reset website

Facebook – Mission Self Reset – Unlock your potential

# References

Research from Southern Methodist University

Duval and Wicklund - *A Theory of Objective Self-Awareness*.

Dan McAdams - North-western University psychology professor

Daniel Goleman – Psychologist (internet information)

Lindsey Agnes (Change your life with NLP)

Thomas Bien – author (internet information)

Richard Davidson - Research from Wisconsin

Indian researchers (The Power of Mindfulness).

Gill Hasson bestselling author of Mindfulness and Emotional Intelligence.

Stephen Covey - The 7 habits of highly effective people"

Irene Rubaum-Keller - psychotherapist /can being self-aware can make you thin?

Brian Tracey – Author (internet information)

• • • • • • • • • • • • • • • • • • • • • • • • • • • • • • • • • • • • • • • •

Printed in Great Britain
by Amazon